GIRLS RECOVERING AS CHRIST EMPOWERS

A Guide for Survivors of Sexual Abuse

Michelle Price

graceministries.life

ISBN: 9798671452440

Cover design by: Jonathan Spann with Adobe Spark
Library of Congress Control Number: 2018675309
Printed in the United States of America

For my mother, Kathy, who taught me how to conquer this valley.

But you, God, see the trouble of the afflicted; you consider their grief and take it in hand. The victims commit themselves to you; you are the helper of the fatherless. You, LORD, hear the desire of the afflicted; you encourage them, and you listen to their cry, defending the fatherless and the oppressed, so that mere earthly mortals will never again strike terror. Psalm 10:14, 17-18

CONTENTS

PREFACE

Once I became a victim of sexual assault, I knew I needed healing but was clueless as to how to go about it. I decided to go to the Christian bookstore to look for resources to guide me in my pursuit. I was disappointed to find very little readily available information. My online search was more fruitful, but I was surprised by the expense of quality support. My goal in writing the GRACE Curriculum is to offer an inexpensive yet quality guide for women seeking healing from sexual abuse.

The healing journey of sexual assault is not a "walk in the park" but an unpredictable and treacherous feat that should not be attempted without adequate support and proper self-care. Use the curriculum at your discretion and do not consider working through it until you are fully prepared to face your hurts. This self-help curriculum is based upon my healing journey, and it is NOT intended to be a substitute for psychotherapy, counseling, hospitalization, cognitive behavioral therapy, or other professional care recommended by a physician, psychiatrist, psychologist, or counselor. Participation in psychotherapy is encouraged while completing the study as the curriculum often highlights issues that need further exploration. Ideally, the curriculum should be used in a small group setting based upon relationships established in confidentiality. Groups allow women to share in the celebration of their victories and to find strength during weaknesses and struggles.

Caring for mind, body, and spirit while addressing hurts from the past is of utmost importance. Regular exercise, adequate sleep, and a healthy diet will ensure the strength of your body. Self-care activities (i.e. yoga, meditation, deep breathing, visualization, adult coloring, listening to music, hiking through the woods, taking a bubble bath, journaling, getting a massage, walking in the park, or speaking with a trustworthy friend) should be planned as a release during emotional triggers. The GRACE Curriculum is based upon God's Word because it is my belief complete healing can only be found at the feet of Jesus. Spending time in prayer, worshipping, and reading the Bible establishes an open connection with the LORD who will guide you along your unique healing journey.

INTRODUCTION

Jesus offers hope and healing for the woman who has suffered from sexual abuse! The task of rebuilding a life after such trauma can feel overwhelming and frightening but ignoring the wounds can have devastating consequences. Sexual abuse has physical, emotional, spiritual, and/or sexual ramifications. Ultimately, many women feel isolated, ashamed, confused, broken, and dejected; but they are not alone. The Department of Justice reports that one in four women are sexually abused and one in six are raped in their lifetime. Unfortunately, victims are often silenced by shame from the violation of their virtue and self-respect. Therefore, the statistic is likely much higher considering only 28% of victims report sexual assault to the proper authorities (The Center for Family Justice).

GRACE Ministries exists to ensure that each woman who has experienced sexual trauma is cherished through life-giving relationships and to develop her understanding of God's grace

while she is transformed into the woman God designed her to be. God's Word says in Ecclesiastes 4:12 that "a person standing alone can be attacked and defeated, but two can stand back-to-back and conquer. Three are even better, for a triple-braided cord is not easily broken." Lasting life change occurs within the framework of relationships. GRACE groups gather a community of believers to support each other in their pursuit of God and the healing He offers.

> *As iron sharpens iron, so a friend sharpens a friend.*
>
> Proverbs 27:17

God rescued us from dead-end alleys and dark dungeons. He's set us up in the kingdom of the Son he loves so much [...] But now, by giving himself completely at the Cross, actually dying for you, Christ brought you over to God's side and put your lives together, whole and holy in his presence. Colossians 1:13, 22

The LORD desires for you to be restored. Author Jenny Swindall reminds us that "the Father always chooses freedom for His kids- it is we who sometimes do not choose it for ourselves" (xvi). God provides this opportunity to pursue deliverance and freedom, but you must choose to commit to the process. Exposing your wounds will be painful and challenging, but the reward far outweighs the risk. Wholeheartedly commit to the next 10 weeks, and we will work together to reclaim the ground the Enemy has taken!

> *Grace has the power to turn despair into hope (15).*
>
> Justin and Lindsey Holcomb

This day I call the heavens and the earth as witnesses against you that I have set before you life and death, blessings and curses. Now choose life, so that you and your children may live. Deuteronomy 30:19

Let's choose life!

A FALLEN WORLD

Why would a good God allow such a horrible thing to happen to me? This is a valid question, and to answer it we must understand the world we live in.

Before the foundation of the world, God created angels to worship Him and carry out His will. They are God's instruments sent to execute His purposes. One of these angels was named Lucifer, and the Bible suggests he was an angel dedicated to worship. Ezekiel 28 describes Lucifer as "perfection, full of wisdom and perfect in beauty," adorned by every precious stone and "anointed as a guardian cherub." Scholars believe Lucifer held the supreme position in the angelic hierarchy and that he guarded the throne of God in heaven (Story of Lucifer). Lucifer became prideful, wicked, and envious of God, and He wanted to take the place of God. The Bible describes Lucifer's change of heart in Ezekiel and Isaiah:

You were blameless in your ways from the day you were created till wickedness was found in you. Through your widespread trade you were filled with violence, and you sinned. [...] Your heart became proud on account of your beauty, and you corrupted your wisdom because of your splendor. Ezekiel 28:15-17

You said in your heart, "I will ascend to the heavens; I will raise my throne above the stars of God; I will sit enthroned on the mount of assembly on the utmost heights of Mount Zaphon. I will ascend above the tops of the clouds; I will make myself like the Most High." Isaiah

14:13-14

The Bible says a war broke out in the heavenlies. God expelled Lucifer from heaven and threw him to earth. In Luke, Jesus describes Lucifer's fall as "lightning from heaven" (Luke 10:18). One-third of the angels followed Lucifer (Revelation 12:4), and he became the "god of this world" (2 Corinthians 4:4). Lucifer, meaning "light-bearer," or "bringing light," was no longer an appropriate name after such a rebellious act. Thus, throughout the Bible, he is referenced by other names more reflective of his character. The Bible describes Satan as a schemer and the "father of lies" (John 8:44). John 10:10 says that Satan comes to "steal and kill and destroy." Therefore, God cautions us to "be alert and of sober mind. Your enemy the devil prowls around like a roaring lion looking for someone to devour" (1 Peter 5:8). Satan's mission is to put a rift between God and man, and he begins pursuing this goal with the very first couple on earth.

> *God is good even when life is bad (9).*
>
> *Robert W. Kellemen*

Read Genesis 1:26-3:6.

Once Eve ate from the tree of the knowledge of good and evil, sin entered the world, and it would never be the same again. When Adam and Eve sinned against God, they relinquished their authority over the world to Satan. Their mistake caused a separation between God and man. People became sinners by nature, and the concept of free will entered creation. Therefore, God allows us to choose voluntarily whether we will follow Him. The apostle Paul describes an inward war going on between his natural tendency to sin and his desire to follow God:

So I find this law at work: Although I want to do good, evil is right there with me. For in my inner being I delight in God's law; but I see another law at work in me, waging war against the law of my mind and making me a prisoner of the law of sin at work within me. What a wretched man I am! Who will rescue me from this body that is subject to death? [...] So then, I myself in my mind am a slave to God's law, but in my sinful nature a slave to the law of sin. Romans 7:21-25

It is because of sin and Satan that Jesus said, "In this world you will have trouble. But take heart! I have overcome the world" (John 16:33). We live in a fallen and violent world, and we must live with the consequences of sin...whether it is ours or someone else's. Sexual abuse occurs because someone else exercises their free will and chooses to sin. Authors Justin and Lindsey Holcomb explain, "The fall and sin invert mutual love and harmony into domination of and violence against each other. Sex, the very expression of human union and peace, becomes a tool for violence after the fall" (Holcomb, 22).

Romans 3:23 says "for all have sinned and fall short of the glory of God." Sin separates us from God, and we fall out of communion with Him, but there is good news!

The Holcombs expound, "Even in this fallen world, God can make all things new. Human depravity cannot stop God's steadfast love from blessing, saving, and restoring all those who trust in him. Despite the actions of sinful people, God's will is accomplished. His good purposes cannot be thwarted (177)."

> *What Jesus has done for you is the answer for what has been done to you (10).*
>
> Pastor Mark Driscoll

God provides a way to end the separation and restore our relationship with Him! John 3:16 tells us "God so loved the world that He gave his one and only Son, that whoever believes in Him shall not perish but have eternal life." Colossians 1:20 explains that "God reconciled everything to Himself. He made peace with everything in heaven and on earth by means of His (Jesus') blood on the cross." Jesus is our gateway to the LORD. The first step toward healing is to begin a relationship with God by accepting Jesus Christ as our LORD and Savior. By acknowledging Jesus' death on the cross as full payment of our sins (past, present,

AND future), our first step toward freedom is taken. We can ask Jesus into our hearts with a simple prayer. First, we must admit we are sinners. Then, we repent and turn from our sins. We must believe in our heart that Jesus Christ lived a perfect life, died on the cross for us, and rose from the grave three days later. Lastly, we can invite Him to become the LORD of our life.

Dear Jesus, thank you for dying on the cross to rescue me from my sins and for establishing a way for me to have a relationship with God. I invite you to come into my heart and to be the LORD of my life. I confess I am a sinner, and I ask for your forgiveness. Fill me with your Holy Spirit to guide and direct my life. I surrender myself to you. In Jesus' name I pray. Amen.

Accepting Christ into our hearts is the most important decision we will ever make in life. We can develop our relationship with Jesus and get to know Him by spending time with Him in the Word and talking to Him throughout the day. We should surround ourselves with other believers who can provide us with accountability and encouragement. As our relationship with Jesus grows, we will want to tell others what Jesus has done in our lives and help others through acts of service.

No one understands what we have been through more than our savior, Jesus Christ, who suffered at the hands of many. He was betrayed, victimized, mocked, beaten, and shamed. How wonderful that we serve a Savior who understands our suffering!

A relationship with Jesus is vital to experience deliverance and freedom; the recovery process is far too difficult without Him. Justin and Lindsey Holcomb enlighten, "the only thing that gets to the depth of the devastation of sexual assault is God's one-way, unconditional love

> *The key to deliverance is knowing the Deliverer.*
>
> *Pastor Chris Hodges*

expressed through, and founded on, the person and redemptive work of Jesus Christ" (Holcomb, 22).

Therapist Dan Allender describes the healing of sexual abuse using the analogy of renovating and restoring a grand old estate that has been abandoned and vandalized:

"The new Owner must be allowed to clean out, repair, redecorate, and live in every room- even those we would rather keep Him out of (14). [...] The fact that our lives are finally given back to God does not mean that every room is immediately restored and beautiful. In fact, it is possible either to refuse to allow God to work on certain rooms, or to be unaware that a secret room might exist on the top floor that needs His attention (5). [...] More is required to deal with the room than merely deeding the property back to God. Specific attention to the damage is required before the restoration is begun (6)."

We will spend the next several weeks walking carefully into every room of our estate. Repairing the house requires hard work, but the result will be built "from God, an eternal house in heaven, not built by human hands" (2 Corinthians 5:1).

Journal

Journaling is an important part of the healing process. Expressive writing leads to emotional, physical, psychological, and spiritual healing. Author of *Writing To Heal*, Dr. James Pennebaker, explains that "when we translate an experience into language we essentially make the experience graspable." Author Thai Nguyen adds, "In doing so, you free yourself from mentally being tangled in traumas." Research has shown that journaling relieves anxiety and stress and induces restorative sleep (Nguyen). Take a few moments to answer the following questions in your journal. Be sure to keep your journal locked or in a safe place where it will not be found.

1. Nobody asks to be sexually abused. However, many women cannot overcome the thought that the abuse is somehow their fault. Do you take on responsibility for what happened to you?

2. Our society often stigmatizes victims of sexual assault and tends to blame traumatized women for their suffering (Holcomb, 41). Has anyone blamed you for what happened to you?

3. What doubts, if any, about God's goodness and care have you struggled with? How have you handled them (Kellemen, 25)?

4. Has your perception of the abuse changed now that you have a better understanding of the world we live in? If so, how?

5. How do you build your relationship with Jesus?

6. Why is journaling important and how can it be helpful?

7. Why do you or don't you think a relationship with God is necessary to heal from sexual abuse?

8. What self-care activities have you committed to doing?

IDENTITY CRISIS

Rock Church, megachurch of San Diego, believes "past sexual abuse [...] is Satan's biggest stronghold over women." Satan uses the experience as a foundation for paralyzing us with fear, anxiety, difficulty concentrating, anger, troubling relationships, sexual dysfunction, and self-worth/identity issues (Rock Church).

Justin and Lindsey Holcomb write, "In the case of severe trauma such as sexual assault, the interpersonal experience of disgrace is internalized. Once internalized, its distorting effects may function apart from the original experience with progressively destructive consequences. Disgrace becomes a core dimension of their identity (53). [...] We'll never peel back enough layers of ourselves to find the true self at the core that is pure and lovable. We need a bigger love to rescue us, one that overcomes the effects of the fall and restores to us the dignity that has been lost. We need a more solid foundation upon which to rebuild identities broken by abuse (81)."

Many of us take on a victim mentality, convincing ourselves that we will never be good enough and will never measure up. Victimization makes us powerless to change, and this is exactly where the Enemy wants us to stay. A survivor of sexual abuse, Kaeley Triller, describes this well:

"In the absence of any tangible sense of value, I drew what felt like the only reasonable conclusion: I was worthless. I spent the next 10 years of my life making heinous choices that perpetuated this lie, until my physical reality matched the condition of my heart."

Like Kaeley, we often allow the past to define our identity, and our behavior and choices reflect it. She describes this "destructive downward spiral" as an "identity crisis," and she believes this is the "tie that binds so many of us together in our sin and shame" (Triller). We won't understand WHO we are until we get to know WHOSE we are.

> *If you are in Christ, your identity is deeper than any of your wounds. [...] Those wounds are not the final word on who you are (80).*
>
> *Justin and Lindsey Holcomb*

Kaeley Triller continues, "While I wasted years of my life waiting for a fairy tale prince to define my sense of worth and identity, a real life King had already stormed the gates of hell to give me a new one. I'm no longer a harlot or a college dropout or a failed wife. I am a daughter of the King."

Our fallen world tries to label us as disgraced, inferior, broken, defiled, dirty, unworthy, damaged, undesirable, unloved, worthless, inadequate, incompetent, unqualified, rejected, unwanted, repulsive, or any number of things. As time progresses, we buy into it and many of us develop feelings of self-contempt. We feel disgusting and condemned, desperate, and powerless to be anything more because we have embraced a false identity. We begin to think we don't deserve a better lot in life and that if we had been a different person the abuse would not have happened to us.

The root of our identity, and ultimately our destiny, lies in our thoughts. American theologian Tyron Edwards once said, "Thoughts lead on to purposes; purposes go forth in action; actions form habits; habits decide character; and character fixes

> *We demolish arguments and every pretension that sets itself up against the knowledge of God, and we take captive every thought to make it obedient to Christ.*
>
> *2 Corinthians 10:5*

our destiny" (Pass It On). If this philosophy is true, then we must change our thoughts, and therefore our behavior, to change our destiny. We must replace the names the world has given us and the lies of the Enemy with the Truth. To embrace our true identity, we must have a thorough knowledge of what God says about who we are.

The Holcombs explain, "What grace offers to the victim experiencing disgrace is the gift of refuting distortions and faulty thinking and replacing their condemning, counterfactual beliefs with more accurate ones that reflect the truths about God, yourself, and God's grace-filled response to your disgrace (45). [...] To experience healing and freedom, your identity must be established on the work of Christ, not on the foundation of the shame and self-hate that frequently results from assault. Making a transition from a 'victim' identity to an identity in Christ is offered in God's redemptive work through Jesus (73)."

Because of our faith in Christ, God's Word says we are...

- Fearfully and wonderfully made

I praise you because I am fearfully and wonderfully made; your works are wonderful, I know that full well. Psalm 139:14

- A conqueror

In all these things we are more than conquerors through Him who loved us. Romans 8:37

- A new creation

Therefore, if anyone is in Christ, he is a new creation; the old has gone, the new has come! 2 Corinthians 5:17

- Holy and blameless

For He chose us in Him before the creation of the world to be holy and blameless in His sight. Ephesians 1:4

- God's child

Yet to all who did receive Him, to those who believed in his name, he gave the right to become children of God. John 1:12

- Christ's friend

I no longer call you servants, because a servant does not know his master's business. Instead, I have called you friends, for everything that I learned from my Father I have made known to you. John 15:15

- A member of Christ's body

Now you are the body of Christ, and each one of you is a part of it. 1 Corinthians 12:27

- A citizen of heaven

But our citizenship is in heaven. And we eagerly await a Savior from there, the LORD Jesus Christ. Philippians 3:20

- The salt and light of the earth

You are the salt of the earth. But if the salt loses its saltiness, how can it be made salty again? It is no longer good for anything, except to be thrown out and trampled underfoot. You are the light of the world. A town built on a hill cannot be hidden. Matthew 5:13-14

- A branch of the true vine, a channel of His life

I am the true vine, and my Father is the gardener. […] I am the vine; you are the branches. If you remain in me and I in you, you will bear much fruit; apart from me you can do nothing. John 15:1, 5

- Chosen and appointed to bear fruit

You did not choose me, but I chose you and appointed you so that you might go and bear fruit- fruit that will last- and so that whatever you ask in my name the Father will give you. John 15:16

- A personal witness of Christ

But you will receive power when the Holy Spirit comes on you; and you will be my witnesses in Jerusalem, and in all Judea and Samaria, and to the ends of the earth. Acts 1:8

- God's temple

Don't you know that you yourselves are God's temple and that God's Spirit dwells in your midst? 1 Corinthians 3:16

- God's workmanship

For we are God's workmanship, created in Christ Jesus to do good works, which God prepared in advance for us to do. Ephesians 2:10

Those who live according to the flesh have their minds set on what the flesh desires; but those who live in accordance with the Spirit have their minds set on what the Spirit desires. The mind governed by the flesh is death, but the mind governed by the Spirit is life and peace. Romans 8:5-6

> *Grace will meet you where you are, but it will never leave you where it found you.*
>
> *Pastor Chris Hodges*

We do not have to have our lives perfectly put together before approaching Jesus! His arms are open wide just waiting for us to come to Him. Justin and Lindsey Holcomb describe God's love for us:

"God loves you now, right now. He doesn't love some future version of you that tries harder, is more obedient, that pays him back for your sins, or that proves that you deserve love. While you were a sinner he died for you because he loved you, and he still loves you now. You have the assurance that you are fully known and fully loved, despite your faults and failings irrespective of how badly others have treated you (117-118)."

We are already princesses and daughters of the Most High King! God made us perfect in His own image, and He loves us unconditionally. Our relationship with

> *God sees greatness in you that you can't see in yourself.*
>
> *Pastor Chris Hodges*

God is not based on OUR worth but the worthiness of Jesus. So, no matter what we have done or *what has happened to us*, when the Father looks at us, He sees His son Jesus! Our identity cannot be shaken because it rests in the hands of God and not on the ebb and flow of life's experiences. As God's daughters, we are righteous, holy, pure, beautiful, innocent, and so much more! We are God's treasured possession.

Finally, [...] sisters, whatever is true, whatever is noble, whatever is right, whatever is pure, whatever is lovely, whatever is admirable-if anything is excellent or praiseworthy-think about such things. Whatever you have learned or received or heard from me, or seen in me-put it into practice. And the God of peace will be with you. Philippians 4:8-9

Journal

1. Describe some of the Enemy's lies you have believed about yourself. What names or labels has the world given you and how does it make you feel?

2. In #1, you identified Satan's lies and the worldly labels you acquired. Use scripture to replace each one with the Truth contained in God's Word.

3. Sexual abuse does not define WHO you are. What steps will you take to learn more about WHOSE you are?

4. Why is it so important for us to escape the victim mentality?

5. How can we re-train ourselves to think thoughts that line up with God's Word?

SHAMED

Following sexual exploitation, victims are often consumed by a destructive storm of confusion, fear, anger, despair, and guilt. Processing these feelings is overwhelming and, ultimately, numbing unless dealt with appropriately. One of the most significant reactions to sexual abuse is shame. Therapist Dan Allender says, "sexual abuse is one of the few crimes that brings more shame to the victim than to the offender. It takes away a person's innocence and self-respect, and usually silences the victim so that help is difficult to find" (1).

Justin and Lindsey Holcomb expound, "Sexual assault is uniquely devastating precisely because it distorts the foundational realities of what it means to be human: embodied personhood is plundered, sexual expression is perverted and used for violence, intrapersonal trust is shattered, and disgrace and shame are heaped on the victim. [...] Sexual assault is a spiritual act in which the connectedness of humans with one another and with God is violated and broken, and the reality of defilement, guilt, terror, shame, alienation, and separation can take years to be made whole again (167)."

Victims of sexual assault experience shame for many reasons. Some women develop a humiliation regarding their sexuality and others feel guilty for experiencing sexual pleasure during the abuse. Many victims are embarrassed by the violation of their innocence. Regardless of the reason, shame is often intensified by the response (or lack of response) by our culture, friends, and family who may attempt to minimize the abuse. The "forget the past and move on" mentality encouraged by those closest to us is ineffective and ultimately a barrier to healing (Holcomb, 21, 55). Addressing shame intentionally is vital because shame separates us from God and makes us powerless to change.

Although many people view them similarly, guilt and shame are very different concepts. Guilt is a feeling about something we have done, but shame is about who we are to the core. Shame is at the root of the identity crisis we discussed in the last chapter, and it has numerous consequences:

- Lying, deception, false pride
- Making unfulfilled promises
- Developing self-worth from the activities we do
- An inability to come to a place of honesty with God and others because we believe we have no true value
- Concentrating on our sin instead of our Savior (Highlands Small Groups, 19)
- Loneliness/isolation
- Becoming a "people-pleaser"

Read Genesis 3:7-12.

Shame caused Adam and Eve to hide from the LORD in the Garden of Eden after eating the forbidden fruit. Like Adam and Eve, shame encourages us to hide who we are and what happened to us from our Father, family, and friends. After trauma, our instincts for self-preservation and survival kick in. In a desperate attempt to protect our heart from further hurts, we deaden ourselves to the pain and build up walls to keep the bad out. At the moment, we are blinded to the fact that our walls also prevent good from coming in.

As you can imagine, the Enemy prefers for us to be ashamed

because shame keeps us from operating in the freedom Christ has for us. The solution to overcome our shame is to view ourselves through God's eyes. Take time to review the material from last week and remember what the Bible says about who we are.

Evil's most scurrilous work is in destroying our passion to love. Evil destroys love by causing us to feel ashamed of our desire to be loved and to love (19).

Robert W. Kellemen

All beautiful you are, my darling; there is no flaw in you. Song of Solomon 4:7

Therefore, there is now no condemnation for those who are found in Christ Jesus.

Romans 8:1

Depending on our own experiences with earthly love, God's love for us may be difficult to understand. If the only love we have encountered in relationships has been dysfunctional, fleeting, selfish, or deceitful, then our understanding of love has been adulterated. God's love is unique and is far greater than any human love. No matter what we have done or will do or what has been done to us, the LORD can never love us more than He does right now. God's love for us is so great that He has numbered the very hairs on our head (Luke 12:7)! His agape love is described perfectly in 1 Corinthians 13:4-8:

Love is patient, love is kind. It does not envy, it does not boast, it is not proud. It does not dishonor others, it is not self-seeking, it is not easily angered, it keeps no record of wrongs. Love does not delight in evil but rejoices with the truth. It always protects, always trusts, always hopes, always perseveres. Love never fails.

1John 4:8 communicates that God IS love. It is intrinsic to all He is and does. And unlike human love that often wanes with distance, God's love for us is boundless and boundary-less. NOT ONE THING can separate us from the love He has for us.

For I am convinced that neither death nor life, neither angels nor demons, neither the present nor the future, nor any powers, neither height nor depth, nor anything else in all creation, will be able to separate us from the love of God that is in Christ Jesus our LORD. Romans 8:38-39

> *At the cross [...] shame and disgrace were transformed into glory and grace (101).*
>
> *Justin and Lindsey Holcomb*

The Bible tells us in Romans 5:8 that God demonstrated His love for us by sending His son to die on the cross to rescue us from our sins. We are all sinners by nature and deserve death, but Christ made the ultimate sacrifice by taking our place on the cross. And because of His death on the cross, shame no longer has power over us! Now THAT is love!

And hope does not put us to shame, because God's love has been poured into our hearts through the Holy Spirit, who has been given to us. Romans 5:5

Journal

1. Miroslav Volf writes (as cited in Holcomb, 2011) in *End of Memory: Remembering Rightly in a Violent World,* "we must name the troubling past truthfully- we must come to clarity about what happened, how we reacted, and how we are reacting to it now- to be freed from its destructive hold on our lives. Granted, truthful naming will not by itself heal memories of wrong suffered: but without truthful naming, all measures we might undertake to heal such memories will remain incomplete (75)." Justin and Lindsey Holcomb add, "Healing begins when the secret is disclosed and the shackles of silence are broken. Healing involves naming evil for what it is and seeing how God rages against it to reestablish shalom (peace) and proclaim his steadfast love for you (63)." Name the past truthfully by describing your sexual abuse in detail...*and the truth will set you free! John 8:32*

*Do not force memories. Sometimes we store or block memories of trauma that may or may not need to be revisited. If you are not prepared to recall the past in the capacity required to answer this question, skip on to the next chapter and consider coming back to it at another time.

2. Have you experienced shame? If so, have you identified the reason for experiencing shame?

3. How have your friends and family responded to your abuse? Did they have a positive, negative, or no response?

4. How do you think our culture has contributed to the shame experienced by sexual abuse victims?

5. Can you think of consequences of shame other than those mentioned in this chapter?

6. Has shame silenced you?

7. Have you built walls around your heart for protection? What good have you potentially missed out on because of these walls? How can you get rid of walls?

8. How have your earthly relationships colored your view of God's love?

FORGIVENESS

Troubles, pains, and offenses are guaranteed in this life because we live in a fallen world. We bury the devastating wounds of sexual abuse deep inside our hearts to function daily. Our enemy jumps at the chance to use the offense to trap us in the bondage of unforgiveness. The reality is that unforgiveness causes emotional and, at times, physical pain.

The Highlands Small Groups team writes, "An offense laced with unforgiveness is like an arrow dipped in poison. The offense slashes through our defenses and hurts us in the moment, but the aftermath of unforgiveness remains long after the event takes place. Its bitter poison seeps into our veins, tainting our thoughts and clouding our vision. If left unchecked, it will eventually penetrate our hearts and paralyze our ability to live, to love, and to be loved. When someone does wrong to us, unforgiveness feels like the right response- after all, shouldn't they have to pay for the offense? But harboring unforgiveness is actually like drinking poison and expecting another person to die (65)."

Forgiveness may seem impossible after what has been done to us. We resist forgiving our abuser because we do not understand what forgiveness is nor the effect that unforgiveness ultimately has on us.

> *Forgiving can lead to proactive behavior in the present, instead of passive wishes from the past (172).*
>
> *Drs. Cloud and Townsend*

Offering forgiveness to our abuser does NOT in any way minimize the offense. Sexual abuse IS wrong, and it IS painful.

We may rationalize unforgiveness because our abuser has not repented or apologized. However, God wants us to forgive our abuser regardless of whether repentance has taken place. The LIFE curriculum explains that while waiting for an apology "we actually become a hostage to the very one who has wronged us because it leaves our freedom up to another person. Reconciliation takes two, but forgiveness is a one-player game" (Highlands Small Groups, 67).

When we choose to hold our abuser in unforgiveness, we choose to focus on the abuser instead of the one who died to heal us from our abuse.

Forgiveness is NOT an attempt to forget what happened to us because the truth is that we may never forget about our abuse nor our abuser. Our enemy will remind us of the assault so that we harbor bitterness and anger in our hearts. However, God can heal our deep wounds so that when we recall the offense, we do not re-live the pain of the experience.

Forgiveness is also NOT an attempt to allow your abuser freedom from responsibility for their actions. The Holcombs note:

"Forgiveness does not mean that you do not participate in activities that impose consequences on evil behavior such as calling the police, filing reports, church discipline, criminal proceedings, etc. (136)."

Forgiveness does NOT require reconciliation as this may be dangerous in many cases of sexual abuse. The choice you make in your heart to forgive is far more important than trying to notify your abuser that you have made the decision. God will lead you toward reconciliation if it is the path He would like you to follow.

We may struggle to forgive our abuser because we do not think it is fair that they should, in a sense, be "let off the hook." The violation seems so severe that we may believe the abuser does not deserve forgiveness. However, we must surrender the experience to the LORD and trust that He will bring justice. Our abuser sinned against God when he/she hurt us. Giving our anger to God is an expression of faith that He who is the righteous judge will avenge us.

> *Do not repay anyone evil for evil. Be careful to do what is right in the eyes of everyone. If it is possible, as far as it depends on you, live at peace with everyone. Do not take revenge, my dear friends, but leave room for God's wrath, for it is written: "It is mine to avenge; I will repay," says the LORD. On the contrary: "If your enemy is hungry, feed him; if he is thirsty, give him something to drink. In doing this, you will heap burning coals on his head." Do not be overcome by evil, but overcome evil with good.*
>
> *Romans 12:17-21*

And will not God bring about justice for His chosen ones, who cry out to Him day and night? Will He keep putting them off? I tell you, He will see that they get justice, and quickly. Luke 18:7-8

We forgive others not because they deserve it but because He deserves it!

We empower our abuser by allowing the abuse to cripple our future. But we have a choice in how we respond to the abuse. We must get to a point where we decide to take responsibility for our own lives no matter what has happened to us. As we surrender our lives completely to Christ, we can become un-offendable. Others are unable to take advantage of us because we no longer live for man but the LORD (Highlands Small Groups, 24).

All the counseling in the world will not give us the ability to forgive a person who has hurt us so deeply; only the LORD can do that. Surrendering the offense to the LORD is certainly not easy. However, it is possible with the supernatural power of the Holy Spirit. Philippians 4:13 says, "I can do all things through Him who strengthens me." We must not measure our circumstance by our strength because we are weak, but we must rely on the mighty power and strength of the Almighty. Regardless of how critical our circumstances, God's grace is available and sufficient for every believer.

But He said to me, "My grace is sufficient for you, for my power is made perfect in weakness." Therefore I will boast all the more gladly of my weaknesses, so that the power of Christ may rest upon me. 2 Corinthians 12:9

We may never *feel* like forgiving our abuser. Forgiveness is NOT a feeling but a choice. And, for a while, it may have to be a daily choice. We are responsible for our feelings and, ultimately, we are the only ones that can decide to allow God to heal our heart by choosing forgiveness.

Justin and Lindsey Holcomb express, "Grace is the miracle that causes change. It creates loving people who are empowered by the Spirit to do good in this world of hostility and evil. As sinners who have received mercy instead of wrath, we have the otherwise inexplicable capability simultaneously to hate wrong and to give love to those who do wrong. It is a miracle for a sinner to forgive another sinner. But this miracle is based on the prior miracle of God freely offering his Son to bear the wrath deserved by the guilty (133)."

If we are struggling in our pursuit of forgiveness, we must consider the degree to which the LORD has forgiven us. Jesus died on the cross to save us from our past, present, and future sins. He not only forgives our sin and removes it "as far as the east is from the west" (Psalm 103:12) but He also "remembers your sins no more (Isaiah 43:25)." He has extended an unbelievable amount of grace and mercy to us, and He expects us to do the same for others. The

Holcombs explain, "What God did for us [...] opens up a relationship of love and a future of hope. Tenderheartedness flows from a heart overwhelmed with being loved undeservedly and being secured eternally" (134).

> *Holding on to an offense is essentially saying that we have a right to withhold grace from someone (62). [...] We will never have to forgive others more than what God has forgiven us (73).*
>
> *Highlands Small Groups*

Get rid of all bitterness, rage and anger, brawling and slander; along with every form of malice. Be kind and compassionate to one another, forgiving each other, just as in Christ God forgave you. Ephesians 4:31-32

Forgiveness is a command from God. Matthew 6:15 tells us, "But if you do not forgive others their sins, your Father will not forgive your sins." Forgiveness becomes easier once we grasp the weight of the debt the LORD removed for us. Similarly, loving people becomes easier once we experience the abounding love of the Father.

> *Our forgiveness of others becomes an act of worship that we would not enter into except for who He is and for the overwhelming debt of love we owe Him.*
>
> *Anne Graham Lotz*

Love your enemies, do good to those who hate you, bless those who curse you, pray for those who abuse you. Luke 6:27-28

Forgiveness is more than just a decision to move on; it's choosing to love our enemies. Step forward in faith today and start walking in the way of forgiveness. Begin praying for your abuser and ask the LORD to bless him/her. This is one of the hardest things we will do in the healing process, but the reward is great. Forgiveness releases us from the "anger, resentment, hatred, and bitterness that destroy" us (Holcomb, 138).

Lewis B. Smedes illustrates, "To forgive is to set a prisoner free and discover that the prisoner was you."

> *Withholding forgiveness from yourself is essentially communicating to God that Jesus's death on the cross is not enough to cover your past.*

Equally important as forgiving others is forgiveness of self. As we learned earlier, many sexual abuse victims take on responsibility for the offense. Unfortunately, our culture tends to blame the victim instead of the abuser. However, sexual abuse is NEVER the victim's fault. We often give ourselves less grace than we offer to others. After the assault, many women try to reason with "If only I had not worn ___" or "If only I had not gone to ___" or "If only I had listened to ___" or "If only I had known ___." Nothing we did caused the assault to happen and continuing to own the experience will only delay our healing.

The author of Forgiving Yourself describes, "The energy it takes to harbor anger, hatred, and resentment towards yourself is exhaustive. Every bit of energy we give to [...] dwelling on regrets robs us of the energy we need to become the person God wants us to be. [...] Forgiveness is a choice that takes courage and strength, and it gives us the opportunity to become an overcomer rather than remaining a victim of our own scorn. [...] The longer you avoid forgiving yourself, the longer you allow yourself to harbor the feelings that you deserve to suffer [...]. The reality is that you cannot change what has happened. You cannot restore lives to where they were before the event. However, you can make a difference in the lives of others. You can give back [...] by finding a different place to invest your time and compassion. Forgive yourself and let the healing begin!"

Journal

1. How were you wronged, and how do you feel about it?

2. It is important to release your emotions rather than allowing them to boil inside your heart. Write a letter to your abuser expressing how you feel and voicing anything that needs to be said for forgiveness to occur and healing to take place. (You will not be asked to send this letter.)

3. Did you know that forgiveness is commanded by God?

4. Has your abuser apologized to you?

5. Did your abuser take responsibility for their actions or have finite consequences (church discipline, police reports, criminal proceedings, etc.) for their actions?

6. Have you pursued reconciliation with your abuser?

7. When you recall the abuse, do you re-live the pain of the experience?

8. What does it mean to become un-offendable in Christ?

9. How can you make a daily choice to forgive your abuser?

10. Have you forgiven your abuser? Why or why not?

11. Have you forgiven yourself? Why or why not?

12. How can you be praying for your abuser?

AN ONGOING BATTLE

The person that abused you is not your enemy. "People are not our enemy, the devil is. [...] If it is true that hurting people hurt people, then the guilty have their own story as well. Our goal should be to love people and hate the devil" (Highlands Small Groups, 74).

For our struggle is not against flesh and blood, but against the rulers, against the authorities, against the powers of this dark world and against the spiritual forces of evil in the heavenly realms. Ephesians 6:12

The devil is more actively involved in trying to destroy you than you are in resisting him.

Pastor Chris Hodges

Satan's demons and God's angels are fighting a war in the heavenlies. As Christians, we are already on the winning side of that war, but we have a very real enemy to overcome. The Bible tells us to "be alert and of sober mind. Your enemy the devil prowls around like a roaring lion looking for someone to devour" (1 Peter 5:8). Hope follows in the very next verse: "Resist him, standing firm in the faith [...] and the God of all grace, who called you to his eternal glory in Christ [...] will restore you and make you strong, firm and steadfast." (1 Peter 5:9-10).

Much of the wrong we encounter in this world is a consequence of sin, either our own or someone else's. Some of our experiences are orchestrated by the devil himself. If we take our eyes off Christ, we become vulnerable to Satan's lure and can become trapped and taken captive by the Enemy to do his will. The apostle Paul explains:

Opponents must be gently instructed, in the hope that God will grant them repentance leading them to a knowledge of the truth, and that they will come to their senses and escape from the trap of the devil, who has taken them captive to do his will. 2 Timothy 2:25-26

> *Satan loves to feed our distrust of God with betrayal by those who ought to be trustworthy (12).*
>
> *Robert W. Kellemen*

Whether we realize it or not, Satan is actively involved in our lives, and he has plans for us. He tempts, lies, opposes, accuses, and slanders us in such a way that we become so engrossed in the devastation that we question or lose our faith and doubt both our purpose and value. When this occurs, we fail to fulfill the plan that God ordained for our lives from before the very foundation of the world.

Ephesians 6:16 says that the evil one fires flaming arrows at us. His expertise from centuries of practice, coupled with his observation of our behaviors and reactions, enables him to fire flaming arrows directly at our open wounds. He is deliberate and crafty, and he knows very well the areas in which we are the most vulnerable.

> *Satan and his demons continue to speak words of rebellion to our minds. If we aren't enlightened to this truth, we will be his advocate in hurting others and even ourselves with the words we speak (87).*
>
> *Highlands Small Groups*

The Achilles' heel for many of us is the injury originating from our sexual abuse. If he has not already, the devil will attempt to use the abuse to paralyze our effectiveness for the kingdom of God. The Enemy uses our vulnerability during suffering to convince us that we deserved what happened to us. He seizes the opportunity to define us by the assault, and he calls us "victim" and "defiled." At the moment, we may not recognize the devil for who he is, and we buy into the thoughts of condemnation and self-contempt he places into our minds.

Beth Moore states, "There is no time I'm more vulnerable to the enemy's attack than when I'm suffering because he knows I'm weak and I'm hurting and I'm prone to believe something that is not true. Self-loathing...self-condemnation...doubt. I'm wild game to the enemy."

The Bible says we should take these thoughts captive:

For though we live in the world, we do not wage war as the world does. The weapons we fight with are not the weapons of the world. On the contrary, they have divine power to demolish strongholds. We demolish arguments and every pretension that sets itself up against the knowledge of God, and we take captive every thought to make it obedient to Christ. 2 Corinthians 10:3-5

Although our enemy is at work we do not need to fear him. 1 John 4:4 says, "the one who is in you is greater than the one who is in the world." The Bible says in 2 Timothy 1:7 that "God has not given us a spirit of fear and timidity, but of power, love, and self-discipline."

> *Such love has no fear, because perfect love expels all fear.*
>
> *1 John 4:18*

Luke 10:17 says in the name of Jesus even the demons are subject to us. When God is with us, the Enemy does not stand a chance! God has equipped us, and we can prepare for battle by putting on the armor of God when we wake up every morning.

Finally, be strong in the LORD and his mighty power. Put on the full armor of God, so that you can take your stand against the devil's schemes. [...] Therefore put on the full armor of God, so that when the day of evil comes, you may be able to stand your ground, and after you have done everything, to stand. Stand firm then, with the belt of truth buckled around your waist, with the breastplate of righteousness in place, and with your feet fitted with the readiness that comes from the gospel of peace. In addition to all this, take up the shield of faith, with which you can extinguish all the flaming arrows of the evil one. Take the helmet of salvation and the sword of the Spirit, which is the word of God. Ephesians 6:10-17

With the armor of God in place, we are ready to be a mighty warrior for the LORD!

We must submit to the authority of Jesus every day and close any open doors that give the devil access to our lives. If we are involved in sin, we must confront it quickly and repent so the Enemy does not gain a stronghold. When we spend time in the LORD's presence daily, we are not only actively engaged in warfare but are also placing ourselves beneath God's protective covering.

The Highlands Small Groups team explains, "When you give God your high praises, it is warfare against Satan. When we give God all our attention, we strip the enemy of any power over our souls and bodies. In His presence, we are protected from all the schemes of the enemy (136)."

Although our enemy attempts to harm us by our abuse, there is good news! The Bible says that "in *all things* God works for the good of those who love him, who have been called according to his purpose" (Romans 8:28). The devil intended to harm us, "but God intended it for good to accomplish what is now being done, the saving of many lives" (Genesis 50:20). We may never know why the abuse happened to us, but in Christ, there is FULL redemption!

The great evangelist Billy Graham once said, "Comfort and prosperity have never enriched the world as adversity has done. Out of pain and problems have come the sweetest songs, the most poignant poems, the most gripping stories. Out of suffering and tears have come the greatest spirits and the most blessed lives."

Imagine the potential we have to advance the kingdom of God when we fully surrender our lives to Jesus and are filled from head to toe with the Holy Spirit. Jesus said we will do even greater things than He did!

Very truly I tell you, whoever believes in me will do the works I have been doing, and they will do even greater things than these, because I am going to the Father. John 14:12

God has filled those who believe in Jesus with His might and power. Jesus said in Matthew 17:20 that if we have faith as small as a mustard seed then we can move mountains, and nothing will be impossible for us!

I ask that the eyes of your heart may be enlightened, so that you may know the hope of His calling, the riches of His glorious inheritance in the saints, and the surpassing greatness of His power to us who believe. He displayed this power in the working of His mighty strength which He exerted in Christ when He raised Him from the dead and seated Him at His right hand in the heavenly realms. Ephesians 1:18-20

Journal

1. "If it is true that hurting people hurt people, then the guilty have their own story as well (Highlands Small Groups, 74)." Have you ever considered that your abuser has a story? Does this change your perception of him/her? If so, how?

2. In what ways has the Enemy defined you by the abuse?

3. How can you actively resist the devil?

4. How can sin become a stronghold in our lives?

5. Have you doubted your purpose and value because of the abuse? If so, how?

6. What are practical ways we can take our thoughts captive and make them obedient to Christ?

7. How is God working out the abuse for your good and His glory?

OUR HEALER

Sexual abuse injures our mind, body, and spirit with a myriad of short- and long-term consequences. Common physical injuries include bruising, bleeding, trouble walking, physical discomfort, and broken or dislocated bones. Long term physical effects may consist of sexually transmitted infections, unwanted pregnancies, or even complications of internal damage. For some of us, emotional damage causes physical manifestations such as fatigue, chest pain, shortness of breath, stiff muscles, uncontrollable shaking or even seizures, unhealthy eating or sleeping patterns, GI upset, sexual dysfunction, infertility, or irregular menstrual cycles.

Less obvious wounds include the effects of trauma on our emotional and spiritual lives. Sexual abuse can change how we believe in God and how we view the world. It may lead to chronic stress, anger and blame, shock, numbness, loss of control, disorientation, helplessness, vulnerability, fear, guilt, insecurity,

or distrust. And many of us suffer psychological effects of abuse such as post-traumatic stress disorder, anxiety, depression, or dissociation (Joyful Heart Foundation). Justin and Lindsey Holcomb explain, "Regardless of how long ago the assault took place, the traces of an assault can reach into the present life of a victim and trigger ongoing problems (37). In order to heal, you need God's compassion and redemptive work applied to your suffering (54)."

> *God has a plan to turn despair into blessings (152).*
>
> *Justin and Lindsey Holcomb*

We have suffered much from the assault, and we should take the time to grieve our losses. The Holcombs expound, "feeling that you lost something, whether your innocence, youth, health, trust, confidence, or sense of safety can lead to despair. Despair invades all areas of life, depriving victims of motivation and sense of purpose. If you've experienced the exhaustion of despair, you've often wondered how you can make it through another day just managing day-to-day life. [...] Despair is the total absence of any sense of hope, accompanied by a feeling of powerlessness. [...] The risk of hope is too great. It seems easier to quit trying and become numb than to have hope dashed again and again. [...] When hope is lost, life becomes mechanical, rote- seeing each day as nothing more than a repetition of what came before (145-146)."

> *Now to Him who is able to do immeasurably more than all we ask or imagine, according to His power that is at work within us.*
>
> *Ephesians 3:20*

However, our grief is not founded on despair but a confident hope that Jesus will utilize our sorrow in our restoration (Holcomb, 61-62). No matter the injury, Jesus Christ offers complete healing of our mind, body, and spirit. We get to decide if we are going to remain in the pain or step forward in faith toward the healing God offers. The LIFE Curriculum notes, "If He only offered us eternal life, it would have been more than enough, but He goes beyond that and offers us *complete* healing and restoration in *every* area of our life" (Highlands Small Groups, 118). Jesus' resurrection is proof that God redeems, heals, and makes all things new. His resurrection not only shows that He has conquered all our enemies but also guarantees that we have a future resurrection to eternal life (Holcomb, 23, 147). His love for us goes beyond rescuing us from death. He desires to touch every broken area of our lives to make us whole and new!

Therefore, if anyone is in Christ, the new creation has come: The old has gone, the new is here! 2 Corinthians 5:17

This image of the conquering Christ who prevailed through suffering can give you hope. In being united to Christ, you, too, will conquer as you look through the eyes of faith to the one who has accomplished everything on your behalf through his death and resurrection (149).

Justin and Lindsey Holcomb

The Bible records multiple accounts of miraculous healings performed by Jesus and His disciples. Matthew 4:23 says Jesus not only proclaimed the good news of the gospel but also healed every disease and sickness. The Gospels document the story of the woman with the issue of blood. She had suffered for twelve years when she encountered Jesus, and she was desperate for healing. She gave the doctors every penny she had, but she continued to worsen. Everything the world had to offer could not save her.

Read Mark 5:25-34.

Mustard seeds are only 1-2 mm in size!

This story provides the perfect example of how we can move mountains when we have faith the size of a mustard seed! Our very small step of faith motivates God to work in the supernatural to make our mountains move (Carrie Wilson). All we must do is believe that God can and *will* act on our behalf! Matthew 14:14 says our LORD heals because He has compassion on us. God wants us to come to Him with our needs and desires. He cares for us, and He desires to heal our hearts.

Hebrews 4:16 says that when we approach God with confidence, we will receive grace and mercy. He wants to do good things for those who have totally surrendered to Him (Lamentations 3:25). God takes care of our needs when we make Him our priority and possess a spirit of openness and humility.

> *But He was pierced for our transgressions, He was crushed for our iniquities; the punishment that brought us peace was on Him, and by His wounds we are healed.*

But seek first His kingdom and His righteousness, and all these things will be given to you as well. Matthew 6:33

God not only responds to a confident faith but to prayer and confession as well.

Therefore confess your sins to each other and pray for each other so that you may be healed. The prayer of a righteous person is powerful and effective. James 5:16

> *The enormity of sin is wildly overwhelmed by the infinite grace of God (30).*
>
> *Robert W. Kellemen*

Even though we are victims of the abuses executed against us, we are still responsible for the sins we have committed as a result of the abuse. Confession can be very difficult because we often worry others may judge us for our sins. However, God does something very powerful in our hearts when we humbly confess our sins to one another. Acknowledgment of our sin brings the darkness to light, breaks the bondage of sin from our lives, and strengthens our spirit. The development of a trustworthy relationship with one of our sisters in Christ not only provides a suitable environment for confession but also for accountability and the opportunity for agreement.

Again, truly I tell you that if two of you on earth agree about anything they ask for, it will be done for them by my Father in heaven. Matthew 18:19

An obstacle to receiving healing is to believe God no longer performs miracles. However, the Bible says in Hebrews 13:8 that

Christ is the same yesterday, today, and forever. In the Psalms, David describes healing as one of the benefits of Christ's sacrifice on the cross:

Praise the LORD, my soul; all my inmost being, praise his holy name. Praise the LORD, my soul, and forget not all his benefits—who forgives all your sins and heals all your diseases, who redeems your life from the pit and crowns you with love and compassion, who satisfies your desires with good things so that your youth is renewed like the eagle's. Psalm 103:1-5

Jehovah Rapha, our healer, redeems and transforms us from victim to overcomer. He utilizes our past to fulfill our destiny!

The LORD does not always heal us instantaneously. In fact, restoration and healing from sexual abuse often take time, and it may take much longer than we expect. However, because Jesus lives in us, our redemption is as certain as His resurrection (Holcomb, 150).

Sometimes God chooses to use medicine to heal. And many times, He decides to heal us once we have joined Him in heaven. No matter the timing, we will all receive a new body when our time on earth is over.

Heal me, O LORD, and I shall be healed; save me, and I shall be saved, for you are my praise.

Jeremiah 17:14

So will it be with the resurrection of the dead. The body that is sown is perishable, it is raised imperishable; it is sown in dishonor, it is raised in glory; it is sown in weakness, it is raised in power; it is sown a natural body, it is raised a spiritual body. 1 Corinthians 15:42-44

We may have difficulty understanding why God would choose not to heal us instantaneously, but the Bible says in Isaiah 55:9 that God's ways are higher than our ways and His thoughts are higher than our thoughts. When we understand God's character,

> *He will wipe every tear from their eyes. There will be no more death or mourning or crying or pain, for the old order of things has passed away.*
>
> *Revelation 21:4*

we can trust and believe His decisions are best. God always has a purpose in the process.

Not only so, but we also glory in our sufferings, because we know that suffering produces perseverance; perseverance, character; and character, hope. And hope does not put us to shame, because God's love has been poured out into our hearts through the Holy Spirit, who has been given to us. Romans 5:3-5

Journal

1. Jesus understands our suffering because He suffered unjustly while sacrificing Himself for us. Write a psalm of lament for the losses you have suffered (Examples: Psalm 6, 13, 22, 142).

2. Many of us believe God is capable of healing but have a hard time believing that He *wants* to heal us. In what areas of your life do you want to receive healing? What might be hindering your ability to receive healing?

3. Do you have a trustworthy friend that may be able to provide a safe environment for confession, accountability, and agreement? If not, how could you find one?

4. What physical, emotional, spiritual, or psychological injuries have you experienced because of your abuse?

5. Do you believe God still performs miracles today?

BOUNDARIES

Sexual abuse invades our privacy and violates our boundaries. As a result, we often have a poor understanding of boundaries, and we may have trouble creating healthy limits in our relationships (Cloud, 36). The purpose of this chapter is to help us understand how boundaries are affected by sexual abuse and to learn how to utilize biblical boundaries appropriately to attain the relationships God always intended for us (28).

Boundaries experts Drs. Cloud and Townsend describe, "Boundaries are personal property lines that define who you are and who you are not, and influence all areas of your life. Physical boundaries help you determine who may touch you and under what circumstances. Mental boundaries give you the freedom to have your own thoughts and opinions. Emotional boundaries help you deal with your own emotions and disengage from the harmful, manipulative emotions of others (front cover)."

The skills necessary for developing healthy boundaries such as saying "no," truth-telling, and respecting personal space are generally learned as a child. The health of the family unit and our childhood experiences ultimately determine whether we will take on the responsibility of self-protection by creating boundaries (181). The foundation of our understanding of who we are is a result of these primary childhood relationships. This explains why children who grow up in loveless homes can be surrounded by loving relationships in adulthood yet believe they are insignificant and unlovable (282).

God wants us to recognize our wounds and shortcomings. We must ask Him to reveal the relationships and life experiences that have contributed to our own boundary struggles (64).

Search me, O God, and know my heart; test me and know my anxious thoughts. See if there is any offensive way in me, and lead me in the way everlasting. Psalm 139:23-24

Drs. Cloud and Townsend explain, "When we have unmet needs, we need to take inventory of these broken places inside and begin to have those needs met in the body of Christ so that we will be strong enough to fight the boundary fights of adult life. These unmet developmental needs are responsible for much of our resistance to setting boundaries. God has designed us to grow up in godly families where parents do the things he has commanded. They nurture us, they have good boundaries, they forgive and help us resolve the split between good and bad, and they empower us to become responsible adults. But many people have not had this experience. They are psychological orphans who need to be adopted and cared for by the body of Christ; to differing extents, this is true of all of us (259)."

Sometimes exploring the deepest parts of our soul produces unanticipated problems such as a resurfacing of traumatic memories, relapsing depression, or relational conflict. We must be careful not to withdraw from meaningful relationships during this time (223). As costly as the consequences of exploring our souls and setting limits seem, it hardly compares to a life lived without a voice and an understanding of who we truly are (253).

Many of us have inverted the function of boundaries to keep the good out and the bad in (34). During a time when we need others most, our inclination is to disconnect from our relation-

> *The more we isolate ourselves, the harder our struggle becomes (224). Isolation guarantees spiritual vulnerability (228).*
>
> *Drs. Cloud and Townsend*

ships due to insecurity, pride, or shame (223). We tend to isolate ourselves from others and hold onto the hurt instead of expressing our pain (34). We shut down emotionally and build walls around our hearts to keep anyone else from hurting us. Many times, we attempt to conceal the pain by denial or minimization, self-destruction, working long hours, developing an addiction to shopping, food, alcohol, drugs, or sex, or any number of other distractions. However, once the mask is removed, our isolation is unbearable and the pain undeniable (227). We must realize that isolation is one of Satan's many strategies. Separation from others allows him a full 360 degrees to prowl around us like a lion seeking to destroy us (1 Peter 5:8). Our most basic need is to live in community with God and others. Jesus teaches this important concept when He describes himself as a vine and us as the branches; He says, "apart from me you can do nothing" (John 15:5).

We may find that after the abuse, we have had trouble accepting and giving love. Jesus says we should "Love the LORD your God with all your heart and with all your soul and with all your mind. This is the first and greatest commandment. And

> *While self-preservation schemes may help you to manage your pain and protect against the nightmare of powerlessness, betrayal, confusion, and rejection, no amount of denial will erase your pain; it only postpones healing (54).*
>
> *Justin and Lindsey Holcomb*

the second is like it: Love your neighbor as yourself" (Matthew 22:37-39). The Bible says that we should "open wide your hearts also" (2 Corinthians 6:11). However, we are unable to give what we do not already have. We must first accept God's love for us before we can begin to accept love from others or reciprocate it. Paul prays this need for the Ephesians when he says, "I pray that you, being rooted and established in love, may have power, together with all the LORD's holy people, to grasp how wide and long and high and deep is the love of Christ, and to know this love that surpasses knowledge—that you may be filled to measure with the fullness of God" (Ephesians 3:17-19). Giving and receiving love is a choice, and we have a responsibility to respond to the love around us (49-50).

> *The past is your ally in repairing your present and ensuring a better future (64).*
>
> *Drs. Cloud and Townsend*

Once we begin setting limits for the first time after a lifetime of compliance or disrespected boundaries, we may experience many emotions including anger toward others and grief over the loss (Cloud, 117). Most abuse victims, if not all, experience anger, and most often our family, friends, culture, and/or religion encourage us to suppress it. Anger does not disappear when we ignore it. If not expressed healthily, anger can consume us and begin to destroy us from the inside out (Holcomb, 125). God says in Ephesians 4:26 that in our anger we should not sin.

Everyone should be quick to listen, slow to speak and slow to become angry. James 1:19

Drs. Cloud and Townsend explain, anger "is the protest of earlier parts of your soul. Those parts need to be unveiled, understood, and loved by God and people. And then you need to take responsibility for healing them and developing better boundaries" (119).

Justin and Lindsey Holcomb expound, "Being consumed with anger slowly erodes the good and life-giving things in your life and starts to cloud your thinking about everyday situations that have nothing to do with why you are angry. [...] Though bitterness and hatred may dull the ache of desperation, hurt, fear, and vulnerability, you've fixed your focus outward rather than inward where the pain resides. [...] Godly anger is healing and redemptive; sinful anger is ugly and vindictive as it gives way to bitterness and hatred. [...] Sinful anger- bitterness, wrath, and anger that wills to harm another- feeds on itself and grows, making situations worse by responding to evil with evil, begetting more evil. [...] Ungodly anger attempts to rectify the wrong done to us by empowering us to act instead of waiting vulnerably for God to do something (126-127, 130-131)."

> *If you do what you are able-*
> *confess, believe, and ask for help-*
> *God will do what you are unable*
> *to do- bring about change (90).*
>
> *Drs. Cloud and Townsend*

As we work through the past, we must get to a point of maturity and begin to establish godly connections with others and learn new patterns of relating to them (98-99, 266). Developing a support network of genuine, intimate, safe, and secure relationships is essential before creating and implementing boundaries. These relationships not only allow us to practice assertiveness in a trusting environment but also to provide a network of wise people we can go to during conflicts with others (66, 115).

Drs. Cloud and Townsend add, "We all need more than God and a best friend. We need a group of supportive relationships. The reason is simple: having more than one person in our lives allows our friends to be human. To be busy. To be unavailable at times. To hurt and have problems of their own. To have time alone (115)."

So where do we get this enveloping foundation? A support system may include a therapy group, counselor, pastor, and/or small group; but our strongest relationships should be with the family of God (171). Jesus says in Matthew 12 "whoever does the will of my Father in heaven is my brother and sister and mother." Great freedom exists in spiritual ties because the relationships are governed by God's standards of honesty, boundaries, responsibility, accountability, healthy confrontation, and forgiveness (138). The family of God proposes to do His will and to love others as He originally designed. When we are properly connected with God and our support network, we are filled with the life and grace we need during crisis and conflict (151).

Drs. Cloud and Townsend note, "Grace must come from the outside of ourselves to be useful and healing. Just as the branch withers without the vine (John 15:1-6), we can sustain neither life nor emotional repair without bonding to God and others. God and his people are the fuel, the energy source from which any problem is addressed. We need to be 'joined and held together by every supporting ligament' (Ephesians 4:16) of the body of Christ to heal and to grow up (224)."

Two are better than one, because they have a good return for their work: If one falls down, his friend can help him up. Ecclesiastes 4:9-10

> *Isolation keeps what is broken in the soul sequestered in the darkness- out of the light of relationship with God and others, where there can be neither help nor resolution (221).*
>
> *Drs. Cloud and Townsend*

The principal step in boundary-setting is openly and honestly communicating our feelings, thoughts, and opinions to others so they have a clear understanding of where we stand and how we define ourselves (37). Drs. Cloud and Townsend say, "because of our fears, we hide aspects of ourselves in the darkness, where the devil has an opportunity." Healing from abuse never takes place in the darkness; it must be brought into the light (104).

Speaking the truth in love, we will grow to become in every respect the mature body of him who is the head, that is, Christ. Ephesians 4:15

Healthy boundaries give direction to our lives and move us closer to fulfilling our personal goals (291). Our yes becomes yes and no becomes no. We are no longer overcommitted and overextended but are one step

> *People tend to look outside of themselves for the problem. This external perspective keeps you a victim. It says that you can never be okay until someone else changes (269).*
>
> *Drs. Cloud and Townsend*

closer to becoming more like Jesus.

For those of us who are recovering singles, we must be careful in dating relationships. We may entrust ourselves too quickly to someone we are dating because of our intense need for safety, acceptance, approval, and love (153). Giving up our boundaries to get love or to avoid abandonment can lead to further exploitive, abusive, or dysfunctional relationships (233). Looking toward human relationships to satisfy our needs will leave us devastated and empty (153); we must look to the LORD to meet our every need. Our satisfaction and fulfillment are found in Christ alone.

Above all else, guard your heart, for everything you do flows from it. Proverbs 4:23

The possibility of reconciliation with our abuser depends on the situation. For some, reconciliation may never be possible, safe, or healthy. During recovery from sexual abuse, we must avoid people who have violated our boundaries. We should tend to our wounds before relationships can be re-established. If our desire for reconciliation is strong, we may find ourselves back in a controlling environment before we are capable of maintaining healthy boundaries (140). We must learn the value of saying "no" to others when setting limits on abuse (36). The primary goal is personal restoration and healing. Reconciliation would be a bonus but is not a required step for healing to occur and a lifetime of fulfillment to be attained.

> *The first step will be the hardest. Go out and do it, and look for his help. Fix your eyes on Jesus, "the author and perfecter" of our faith (Hebrews 12:2) (254).*
>
> Drs. Cloud and Townsend

The reality is that most abusers are not willing to give up control in the relationship and would not respect any newly established boundaries. The abuser must take responsibility for the abuse and then prove trustworthy over time. Repentance is more than an apology; it's producing "fruit in keeping with repentance" (Matthew 3:8) (Cloud, 257).

As we gather the courage to take the first step in setting limits and making changes, we should remember who God is and what He has done for us. God is faithful, trustworthy, and full of mercy and grace. He sent His son, Jesus, for our redemption and future. God is moving in our lives, and our time of deliverance is near for those who persevere (267). God said that we would have trouble in this world, but He is always there to carry us through it (273).

So do not throw away your confidence; it will be richly rewarded. You need to persevere so that when you have done the will of God, you will receive what he has promised. Hebrews 10:35-36

Remember the Serenity Prayer: "God grant me the serenity to accept the things I cannot change, the courage to change the things I can, and the wisdom to know the difference."

Journal

1. How have your boundaries been violated? What relationships and experiences have contributed to your ability or inability to set boundaries?

2. What reward do you get by not setting boundaries (examples include money and relationships)? What might you lose by setting boundaries?

3. Kubler Ross identified 5 stages of grief and loss: denial, anger, bargaining, depression, and acceptance. What stage are you currently experiencing and why?

4. Your support network should be full of relationships characterized by unconditional love. Who is in your network? How could you find quality relationships to develop your network?

5. What do you need? What do those who are closest to you think that you need?

6. How would you describe the health of your family unit?

7. Why do you have to accept God's love before you can learn to be loved or to love others well?

8. How have you tried to conceal your pain?

PURITY

Our abusive sexual encounters encourage a perverted view of sex. We may ultimately draw the conclusion that sex is evil because of what has been done to us. However, God created sexual intimacy to be an enjoyable experience between one man and one woman in a covenant marriage relationship.

All living things are given the desire for sex because of the need to reproduce for the preservation of the species. God wired humans with chemicals in the brain that help to serve this purpose. Our brain stimulates our ovaries to produce estrogen and testosterone which drive our desire for sexual gratification. The pathways of our brain that control "reward" behavior determine our attraction to others. The major chemical responsible for this reward pathway is dopamine, which is produced when we do things that feel good such as engaging in sex, spending time with those we love, and during addictive behavior. A chemical called norepinephrine is also produced during attraction. Interestingly, this is the exact same chemical that plays a role during trauma when the body responds in "fight" or "flight." Lastly, our brain produces oxytocin and vasopressin, chemicals predominantly responsible for long-term attachment, and preservation of the relationship (Katherine Wu). How amazing is it that God designed us to desire sex, enjoy it, and then afterward experience a deepening of the marriage bond?

Sex becomes destructive when it occurs outside of the context God originally intended. Satan understands God's design for sex and the importance of sexual intimacy in marriage. Sexual assault is one of the Enemy's primary means of distorting it (Holcomb, 166). With the natural release of all those chemicals, just imagine the confusion that can occur for the victim of sexual assault! We can experience great uncertainty about our sexuality. Some of us feel guilty because we experienced the natural, pleasurable dopamine surge during the abuse. Others of us associate the "fight" or "flight" response with sex and develop a post-traumatic stress disorder. Some of us question our sexual preference, and many of us often respond to the assault with promiscuity. As young victims, our developmental knowledge concerning sex or intimacy becomes extremely distorted and far from God's truth. What was once a unique and beautiful gift from God has become cheapened and devalued. Ultimately, the Enemy takes advantage of the aftermath of the assault to perpetuate sexual perversion and confusion. We must revert to God's original design for sex that is so beautifully outlined in His Word:

But at the beginning of creation God 'made them male and female.' For this reason a man will leave his father and mother and be united to his wife, and the two will become one flesh. So they are no longer two, but one flesh. Therefore what God has joined together, let no one separate. Mark 10:6-9

Purity is "the quality of being free from what vitiates [spoils], weakens, or pollutes; containing nothing that does not properly belong; free from moral fault or guilt; marked by chastity; ritually clean;" unmixed (Pure).

The Bible records God's offer of hope and healing for our sexuality. Jesus' finished work on the cross restores our purity. We can stand before God "holy," "blameless," and "above reproach" (Colossians 1:22). We are redeemed by God's grace, freed from guilt, strengthened by His power, and declared righteous!

The author of the Highlands Freedom curriculum comments, "You may not feel very special or honorable at this moment, but God sees you this way. You are not defined or limited by your past" (Highlands Small Groups, 120). God makes us brand new (2

Corinthians 5:17), and He desires for us to live our lives as women of purity.

Forget the former things; do not dwell on the past. See, I am doing a new thing! Now it springs up; do you not perceive it? I am making a way in the wilderness and streams in the wasteland. Isaiah 43:18-19

> *The LORD will do a miracle in your life if you will allow Him (120).*
>
> *Highlands Small Groups*

We cannot change our past, but we can decide how we will respond to it. We determine the direction of our future. To maintain a life of purity, we must remember that our body is not our own.

Do you not know that your bodies are temples of the Holy Spirit, who is in you, whom you have received from God? You are not your own; you were bought at a price. Therefore honor God with your bodies. 1 Corinthians 6:19-20

Our bodies belong to the LORD. We were bought with the precious blood of Jesus, and since He has restored our purity, we must protect His beautiful creation. Romans 12:1 says caring for our bodies is an act of worship:

Therefore, I urge you, brothers and sisters, in view of God's mercy, to offer your bodies as a living sacrifice, holy and pleasing to God- this is your true and proper worship.

We can ask the Holy Spirit to reveal anything in our lives that keep us from being pure. David provides an example for us in Psalm 139:23-24:

Search me, God, and know my heart; test me and know my anxious thoughts. See if there is any offensive way in me, and lead me in the way everlasting.

The Holy Spirit gently convicts us of our sin, so we can repent with the ultimate goal of becoming more like Jesus. We need to be careful not to confuse the Holy Spirit's conviction with guilt as this is the Enemy's weapon of condemnation. We must remember that mistakes are inevitable, and God is full of grace and mercy.

Because of the LORD's great love we are not consumed, for his compassions never fail. They are new every morning; great is your faithfulness. Lamentations 3:22-23

The LORD is gracious and compassionate, slow to anger and rich in love. Psalm 145:8

Blessed are the pure in heart, for they shall see God.

Matthew 5:8

Being a woman of purity not only pertains to what we do with our bodies but also to what we allow into our hearts.

Above all else, guard your heart, for everything you do flows from it. Proverbs 4:23

The New Living Translation says that we should guard our hearts above all else because it determines the course of our lives. If we allow sin into our

Create in me a pure heart, O God, and renew a steadfast spirit within me.

Psalm 51:10

hearts through our thought life, entertainment, or the company we choose to keep, then these choices will ultimately determine our future (Carrie Wilson).

Therefore, since we have these promises, dear friends, let us purify ourselves from everything that contaminates body and spirit, perfecting holiness out of reverence for God. 2 Corinthians 7:1

The desires of our flesh are persistent, so we must make a conscious decision every day to commit to following Jesus.

For the grace of God has appeared that offers salvation to all people. It teaches us to say "No" to ungodliness and worldly passions, and to live self-controlled, upright and godly lives in this present age, while we wait for the blessed hope- the appearing of the glory of our great God and Savior, Jesus Christ, who gave Himself for us to redeem us from all wickedness and to purify for Himself a people that are His very own, eager to do what is good. Titus 2:11-14

As we struggle from the attempted attacks of our enemy, we must rely on the truth of God's Word to make it through. Dive into the Word in search of truths to combat the negative thinking concerning ourselves, our past, and our future.

Being a woman of purity is not just about sexual virtue but also about connecting to our purpose, realizing the talents and gifts the LORD has placed inside of us, and then leveraging them for the Kingdom (Highlands Small Groups, 119). 2 Timothy 2:21 explains:

If you keep yourself pure, you will be a utensil God can use for His purpose. Your life will be clean, and you will be ready for the Master to use for every good work.

Next week, we will explore God's unique plan for us by discovering our spiritual gifts and putting them into practice to fulfill the calling of God on our lives.

Journal

1. What does it mean to live a life of purity?

2. Why is it important to live a life of purity? How will you commit to a life of purity?

3. Describe your physical, emotional, and spiritual goals for purity (Carrie Wilson).

4. What practical steps will you take to achieve your goals?

5. How has your sexual abuse changed your view of sex?

FULFILLMENT

God created each one of us for a unique purpose that He ordained from the very beginning of time.

Before I formed you in the womb I knew you, before you were born I set you apart; I appointed you as a prophet to the nations. Jeremiah 1:5

God has a plan for our lives that includes hope and abundance. Jeremiah 29:11 says, "For I know the plans I have for you," declares the LORD, "plans to prosper you and not to harm you, plans to give you hope and a

future." For some of us, discovering our purpose can seem like a daunting task. However, God's Word sums up the purpose of a Christ follower with two simple assignments: to love God and to love others.

'Love the Lord your God with all your heart and with all your soul and with all your mind and with all your strength. The second is this: 'Love your neighbor as yourself.' There is no commandment greater than these. Mark 12:30-31

The Highlands Small Groups team notes, "Though the big vision may seem a bit overwhelming, success will come by simply doing the little things: Spend time with the LORD, and apply Tree of Life living to the decisions you make each day. In this way, you will automatically begin to shine a light before men that drives away darkness and fills a lost, broken, and lonely world with great hope (132)."

> *Our decisions will look different if we live intentionally (122).*
>
> *Highlands Small Groups*

The author of the Highlands Freedom curriculum says, "We must become servants of the LORD before He can fulfill His purpose in us" (Highlands Small Groups, 121). As we pray, worship, and immerse ourselves in God's Word daily, we will be connected to the LORD and prepared to serve when He calls. When we seek God's will through prayer and renew our mind, He is faithful to show us the path He has prepared for us.

Do not conform to the pattern of this world, but be transformed by the renewing of your mind. Then you will be able to test and approve what God's will is—His good, pleasing and perfect will. Romans 12:2

God made each one of us with a unique personality and strategic skills, gifts, and talents to use in service to others. 2 Timothy 1:6 says to "stir up the gift of God which is in you." We

> *The meaning of your life is to find your gift. The purpose of your life is to give it away.*
>
> *Pablo Picasso*

should take the time to discover our gifts and talents and then develop them through research, training, counseling, education, and practice.

Drs. Cloud and Townsend state, "All of us- not only full time ministers- have gifts and talents that we contribute to humanity. We all have a vocation, a 'calling' into service. Wherever we work, whatever we do, we are to do 'unto the LORD' (Col. 3:23) (202). Work is a spiritual activity. In our work we are made in the image of God, who is himself a worker, a manager, a creator, a developer, a steward, and a healer. To be a Christian is to be a co-laborer with God in the community of humanity. By giving to others we find true fulfillment (203)."

Everyone is a genius. But if you judge a fish on its ability to climb a tree, it will live its whole life believing that it is stupid.

Albert Einstein

Ever work on completing a puzzle and in placing the last piece discover there is a piece missing? The picture is not complete without each piece fulfilling its part. God sees the whole picture, and we play a part designed and created specifically for us. Hebrews says in 12:1-2, "Throw off everything that hinders and the sin that so easily entangles. And let us run with perseverance the race marked out for us, fixing our eyes on Jesus, the author and perfecter of our faith." Our edges may be worn or withered but the beauty inside completes God's perfect, heaven-made plan. The piece we contribute to the puzzle of life is a necessary part of the bigger picture.

We cannot allow others to tell us what we are and are not capable of. Our enemy will try to convince us that we are unprepared and ill-equipped to fulfill the calling of God on our life. However, we must remember that God is with us, and He makes the impossible possible.

We must let God be bigger than our limitations, and we will find that He will do the impossible through us.

Carrie Wilson

Gloria Copeland encourages, "I want to tell you something that will take a lot of pressure off you and will release faith action: Whatever your qualifications, the race you have been chosen to run is impossible to finish on your own. God's plans are so big you couldn't possibly do it in your own strength and intelligence. It takes faith in Him to finish the race."

God has already equipped us to do the work He has planned for

God doesn't call the equipped; He equips the called.

Pastor Chris Hodges

us to do. We must believe that He will give us the power we need to finish the race marked out for us. 2 Corinthians 12:9 says that God's grace is sufficient for us and that His power is made perfect in our weakness. We have access to the same power that God used to raise Christ from the dead!

I pray that you will begin to understand how incredibly great His power is to help those who believe Him. It is that same power that raised Christ from the dead and seated Him in the place of honor at God's right hand in heaven. Ephesians 1:19-20

The devil tried to destroy our lives through sexual abuse but because of the resurrection of Jesus, our ruins can come to life! God has far greater plans to transform our story and our lives through His redemptive power to make us fit for the Kingdom's use.

You intended to harm me, but God intended it for good to accomplish what is now being done, the saving of many lives. Genesis 50:20

Beth Moore teaches, "It is to your Father's glory that your life bear much fruit showing yourself to be a disciple of Christ. It is the will of God for you to live an abundant life, fully liberated in Christ, and immensely impactful in your sphere of influence. You are meant to be enormously effective in the world where God has placed you."

God allows us the privilege of serving others and setting them free. [...] God unlocks us from our past and hands us the keys in order to unlock others (118).

Highlands Small Groups

Each one of us will fulfill a unique purpose in this life, but we all share the bond of survivorship that can be utilized to speak life into the desperate victim who is suffering the very same story.

Praise be to the God and Father of our LORD Jesus Christ, the Father of compassion and the God of all comfort, who comforts us in all our troubles, so that we can comfort those in any trouble with the comfort we ourselves receive from God. 2 Corinthians 1:3-4

Drs. Cloud and Townsend express, "It is being able to hear the stories of people who have been there, who have been scared, but who can witness to the fact that you can make it. Listen to their trials, how they have been in your shoes, and how God was faithful to them (265)."

The Spirit of the LORD God is upon me, because the LORD has anointed me to bring good news to the suffering and afflicted. He has sent me to comfort the brokenhearted, to announce liberty to the captives, and to open the eyes of the blind. He has sent me to tell those who mourn that the time of God's favor to them has come, and the day of His wrath to their enemies. To all who mourn in Israel He will give: beauty for ashes; joy instead of mourning; praise instead of heaviness. For God has planted them like strong and graceful oaks for His own glory. And they shall rebuild the ancient ruins, repairing cities long ago destroyed, reviving them though they have lain there many generations. Isaiah 61:1-4

Journal

1. Complete the DISC Personality and Spiritual Gifts Assessment at https://www.arcchurches.com/disc/

2. What is your personality/leadership style?

3. How can you make the most of your personality?

4. What are your spiritual gifts?

5. How can you develop your spiritual gifts?

6. How can you put your spiritual gifts into practice?

7. What is the calling of God on your life? If you are unsure, what can you do to discover your calling?

RESOURCES

Boundaries by Dr. Henry Cloud and Dr. John Townsend

Freedom from Depression by Jenny Swindall

Living in Freedom Every Day by Highlands Small Groups

NEW: A curriculum for women with STDs by Carrie Wilson

Sexual Abuse: Beauty for Ashes by Robert W. Kellemen

When Trust is Lost: Healing for Victims of Sexual Abuse by Dan B. Allender

REFERENCES

Allender, Dan B. *When Trust is Lost: Healing for Victims of Sexual Abuse.* Grand Rapids, MI: RBC Ministries, 2010.

Cloud, Henry and John Townsend. *Boundaries.* Grand Rapids, MI: Zondervan, 1992.

"Forgiving yourself." (2002). Retrieved from http://www.all-aboutgod.com/forgiving-yourself.htm

Graham, Billy. *Unto the Hills.* Siloam Springs, AR, 2005.

Harrison, R.K. (1996). Angel. Retrieved from http://www.bible-studytools.com/dictionary/angel/

Highlands Small Groups. *Living in Freedom Everyday: Life Small Group Workbook.*

Holcomb, Justin S. and Lindsey A. Holcomb. *Rid of My Disgrace: Hope and Healing for Victims of Sexual Assault.* Wheaton, IL: Crossway, 2011.

Joyful Heart Foundation. (2016). Effects of Sexual Assault and Rape. Retrieved from http://www.joyfulheartfoundation.org/learn/sexual-assault-rape/effects-sexual-assault-and-rape

Kellemen, Robert W. *Sexual Abuse: Beauty for Ashes.* Phillipsburg, NJ: P&R Publishing, 2013.

Lotz, Anne G. (2004). Joy of My Heart: Forgiveness- An Act of Worship. In Just Give Me Jesus. Retrieved from http://www.christianity.com/devotionals/joy-of-my-heart-with-anne-graham-lotz/joy-of-my-heart-with-anne-graham-lotz-april-3.html

Nguyen, Thai. (2015, April 15). 10 Surprising Benefits You'll Get From Keeping a Journal. Retrieved from http://www.huffington-post.com/thai-nguyen/benefits-of-journaling-_b_6648884.html

"Pass It On." (n.d.) Retrieved from https://www.values.com/inspirational-quotes/4921-thoughts-lead-on-to-purposes-purposes-go-forth

Pure. (n.d.). In *Merriam-Webster Dictionary* online. Retrieved from https://www.merriam-webster.com/dictionary/pure

Rock Church. (2017). Breaking Free. Retrieved from http://www.sdrock.com/events/15414/

"Story of Lucifer." (2002). Retrieved from http://www.allabout-god.com/story-of-lucifer.htm

Swindall, Jenny. *Freedom From Depression*. Lake Mary, FL: Charisma House, 2013.

The Center for Family Justice. (n.d.). Statistics. Retrieved from https://centerforfamilyjustice.org/community-education/statistics/

Triller, Kaeley. (2017, January 16). Bathroom Rules Must Protect, Not Enable. Retrieved from https://billygraham.org/decision-magazine/january-2017/bathroom-rules-must-protect-not-enable/#

US Department of Justice NSOPW. (n.d.). Learn the Warning Signs: Recognizing Sexual Abuse. Retrieved from https://www.nsopw.gov/en-US/Education/RecognizingSexualAbuse?AspxAutoDetectCookieSupport=1

Wilson, Carrie. *NEW*.

Wu, Katherine. (2017, February 14). Love, Actually: The science behind lust, attraction, and companionship. Retrieved from http://sitn.hms.harvard.edu/flash/2017/love-actually-science-behind-lust-attraction-companionship/

ACKNOWLEDGEMENTS

First and foremost, I want to thank God for making beauty out of my ashes. He has truly shown Himself as Redeemer in every aspect of my life. I am beyond grateful He chose me to write this curriculum and to establish GRACE Ministries as a resource for so many hurting women.

I appreciate my wonderful husband and partner in life, Whit Price, who has supported and encouraged me throughout the writing process and has played an integral role in my healing. Thank you for allowing me to invest so much of my time into this project when I could have been spending it with our family.

Thank you to my beautiful daughter, Anna Whitney. Your smiles and coos have encouraged me to be the best person I can be and have reminded me about what is important in life. I pray divine protection over you in this broken world. May you grow up lacking nothing. Your parents love you more than anything in creation.

Thanks to my friends and former Highlands College graduates, Courtney McCulley and Jeannie Nearing, for planting the seeds that ultimately grew into the GRACE Curriculum and GRACE Ministries. I enjoyed working on the school project with you and have been in awe of the work God has done to make it a reality.

I never would have accomplished this feat if it were not for my Freedom leaders, Alicia Pannell and Erin Burnell, who contributed to my spiritual growth and walked alongside me as I navigated the pathway of my healing journey. Thank you for believing in me when I did not believe in myself and for praying over me day in and day out.

A special thank you to my family for their love and support over the years. I am especially grateful to my mother, Kathryn Spenney, and sister, Marian Lorimer, for their assistance with editing and to Jonathan Spann for design and reformatting.

Thank you to my mother's Hunter Street Baptist Church prayer group who spent countless hours praying for me as I navigated the valleys of my life. Your prayers were certainly felt and appreciated in more ways than you know. What a comfort it is to know I have so many prayer warriors standing with me!

I appreciate Erica Russell for believing in the curriculum enough to launch her own GRACE Group. Thanks for giving your time to invest in the hurting.

There are so many others I am grateful for who have invested in me throughout the years including all my friends and fellow small group members. I wish I had enough pages to thank every single one of you by name. I would not be the woman I am today without all of you!